MAD AT MILES:
A BLACKWOMAN'S GUIDE TO TRUTH

By Pearl Cleage

A Cleage Group Publication

For Deignan and Hugh, the next wave.
And for Zaron, the next rave.

MAD AT MILES: A BLACKWOMAN'S GUIDE TO TRUTH is a publication of the Contemporary Division of The Cleage Group, Inc., an independent African-American publishing company. The work in this book was developed with the additional creative and financial support of Just Us Theater Company / Club Zebra, in Atlanta, Georgia.

"In My Solitude" first appeared in ESSENCE Magazine in February, 1989, and is re-printed here with permission.

Special thanks to Henry W. Cleage for advice and counsel; to Bill Bagwell for his friendship and faith; and to Walter R. Huntley, Jr., Cecelia Corbin Hunter, Ingrid Saunders Jones, Melanie E. Lomax, Esq., Kristin Cleage Williams, Johnnetta Cole, Susan Taylor and Haki Madhubuti for their continuing support of my work.

Design by Wayne Sizemore. Cover Photograph by Barry Forbus. Typesetting by ITG, Inc.

"The Blackman's Guide To Understanding the Black Woman" © 1990 Civilized Publications
"Miles: The Autobiography" © 1989 Simon & Schuster

ISBN 0-9628142-0-2

The Cleage Group, Inc.
Evergreen Plaza Suite 326
19785 West Twelve Mile Road
Southfield, Michigan 48076

To order additional copies call: 1-800-325-6524

THE PROBLEM

"When she [the black woman] crosses this line and becomes viciously insulting it is time for the Blackman to soundly slap her in the mouth... She may also have to be physically restrained until her anger and shock passes. It's okay to restrain her, she won't burst and no Blackwoman can win a physical fight against a right Blackman... Soon she will become trained and curb her vicious tongue when talking to him... She'll cry and scream and scratch like a wild animal -- and she must be dealt with as such."

Shahrazad Ali in
"The Blackman's Guide To
Understanding the Black Woman"

"After the first show, I changed clothes, and on my way out Tina was standing close to the door, and she screamed at me," Ike recalls. *"I said 'Don't talk to me like that,' and it was just WHACK!"* He claps his hands hard for emphasis. *"I wasn't even thinking, because she was screaming, and I can't stand for a woman to scream at me, man, I swear to God, man."*

When it was time for the next performance, he says, *"She came onstage -- she's a strong woman, man -- she did the whole show. Afterwards, I said, 'Where you wanna eat?' She said, 'Ike, take me to the hospital. I think my jaw is broke!' She did the whole show without me being able to detect it."*

Ike Turner quoted in People
Magazine, Sept. 3, 1990.

"Cecily's like two different women, one nice, the other one totally fucked up. And she had some friends who I couldn't stand. One time we argued about one friend in particular, and I just slapped the shit out of her."

Miles Davis with Quincy Troupe
"Miles: The Autobiography"

THE SOLUTION

1. WHY I WRITE ... *you have a right to know*

2. IN THE TIME BEFORE THE MEN CAME... *dreams of freedom and the high price of being distracted*

3. MAD AT MILES ... *can they hit us and still be our heroes?*

4. LAST DAY OF THE YEAR ... *life on the front lines*

5. THE OTHER FACTS OF LIFE ... *the things your mother didn't know how to tell you*

6. BASIC TRAINING: THE BEGINNINGS OF WISDOM ... *a new way of talking*

7. IN MY SOLITUDE ... *when we want to be alone*

8. GOOD BROTHER BLUES ... *toward a new definition of manhood*

9. MEAN TO BE FREE ... *a poem for you*

WHY I WRITE: AN INTRODUCTION

Yesterday, as I was writing this, my neighbor, my sister, had to call the police to protect her from her husband, also my neighbor and my brother, who was threatening to douse them both with gasoline and light it in a murder/suicide if she did not stop divorce proceedings and come back to be his wife.

Last week after class, one of my students waited for me to confess softly that her boyfriend had been beating her and what should she do?

A month ago, a young friend who teaches preschool read to me from her journals a harrowing description of the night her former lover shot himself in the head after she escaped from his apartment following months of beating and torture.

My friend the corporate executive relates a story of leaping from a speeding car and running into some urban woods after her husband placed a gun to her temple while driving with her down a busy suburban street.

My friend the well respected public servant comes to work with sunglasses to hide the two black eyes her husband gave her by beating her head against the wall while their children slept in the next room.

My sisterwriter with the three young children tells horror stories of being scalded with boiled water and forced to suck the barrel of a gun as if it was her husbands penis.

And my memory of my own nightmare as an undergraduate student at Howard University, listening to my boyfriend tell me I'd better not move as he tied my hands and feet and told me if he couldn't have me, nobody could.

But that's not all. I also remember the chorus of black male objections to Ntozake Shange's *For Colored Girls.* I hear the protests over Alice Walker's *The Color Purple*, and I remember the forums whining about negative images of black men in *The Women of Brewster Place*, and I wonder where those same black male voices are when black male violence is being condoned and taught and glamorized and ignored. I wonder when we are going to see the same commitment to fighting sexism in the work of our brotherwriters that we see to fighting racism. I wonder how much good all those poems about beautiful African queens can do in the face of a backhand slap across the mouth and a merciless rape in the bedroom of your own house.

I wonder why Haki Madhubuti and Zaron Burnett and Donald Stone are the exceptions and not the rule when their works focus on black male responsibility for admitting to and then stopping the war that is being waged against black women and children by the men who should be our closest allies and most ardent advocates.

But one thing I do not wonder about anymore is why I am writing and what concerns shape and focus my politics, my aesthetics, my form and my content. I remember exactly when it became clear to me.

It was my birthday. My 41st birthday, to be exact. And it began like any other day with me stumbling out of bed to wake my daughter, wishing it wasn't still dark outside in the winter when you have to get up early and wondering what to fix for breakfast. The breakfast question led me into the kitchen where I flipped on the morning news to be sure my country had not invaded somebody while I was sleeping. That's when I heard it.

"A lone gunman, armed with an automatic weapon, opened fire on a group of female students in Montreal, killing 14 and wounding 13 others. The man, who apparently had a grudge against women, shouted, "You're all feminists!" before firing point blank into a group of female students."

The anchorwoman read the copy with the bland unconcern that is her trademark and then went on to tell me about the approach of a winter storm. But I didn't hear it. I was stunned. What kind of murderer was this? Was he angry enough at feminism to pick a random bunch of young women and shoot them down in cold blood? I was angry and frightened and confused.

When I got the morning paper, it didn't do much to reassure me. Photographs on the front page showed wounded women being carried out of the classroom building where they had been shot. Their friends huddled around in small, weeping groups, trying to understand and cope with their grief. A policeman called to the scene found his own daughter among the dead and dying. A male student who survived said, "I heard the gunman say, 'I want the women!' He separated us into two groups, the guys in one corner and the girls in another. When that was done, he asked the guys to leave and then he just started shooting."

I got through the rest of my morning routine, although I don't know how. My daughter shared my shock and horror at what had happened and although I saw the questions in her eyes, I didn't have the reassuring answers that mothers are always supposed to have, no matter what. I didn't have any way to explain to her what this kind of killing was about. I didn't even have a way to explain it to myself yet. It was just scary.

I spent the day looking for news about the gunman and hoping I wouldn't find it. I watched the television broadcasts, listened to the radio reports and made sure I got the afternoon paper for any updated information, but it didn't help me understand more or feel any better. Finally, I had to admit to myself that I wasn't really looking for any explanations. I was looking for a news bulletin that said it was all a mistake. That it had never happened. That a crazy man had not chosen as his target women he identified as feminists, whether they identified themselves that way or not.

By the end of the day, I had to admit that no bulletin was forthcoming. The facts and the death toll remained as grim as they had been when I first heard them on the morning news. The only question that remained was what I was going to do about it.

I was at a loss as to what the correct response should be. I am not a violent person. I own no weapons and have never been in a fight in my life. I am not an organizer and I have no troops to marshal with marching songs and battle plans. What I do is write about what I see and what I feel and what I know in the hope that it will help the people who read it see more and feel more and know more.

It was clear to me by nightfall that the only question I had to answer in the face of the act of war committed against women in Montreal was why I am writing. So I said a prayer for my fallen sisters and for the five women who are murdered in America every day by their husbands or ex-husbands or boyfriends and tried to answer the question as honestly as I could so I wouldn't forget it when there were no headlines or front page horror stories to remind me.

I am writing to expose and explore the point where racism and sexism meet. I am writing to help myself understand the full effects of being black and female in a culture that is both racist and sexist. I am writing to try and communicate that information to my sisters first and then to any brothers of good will and honest intent who will take the time to listen. I am writing because five women a day are murdered by the men who say they love them. I am writing because rape is. I am writing because I am a daughter and a mother and a lover and a sister and a womanist. I am writing to understand. I am writing so I won't be afraid. I am writing so I won't start crying again. I am writing because nobody even said the word sexism to me until I was thirty years old and I want to know why.

I am writing because I have seen my friends bleed to death from illegal abortions. I am writing because I have seen my sisters tortured and tormented by the fathers of their children. I am writing because I almost married a man who beat me regularly and with no remorse. I am writing because my daughter is almost old enough to start "dating" and I don't know how to tell her to protect herself from what I cannot even fully articulate to myself.

I am writing to allow myself to feel the anger. I am writing to keep from running toward it or away from it or into anybody's arms. I am writing to find solutions and pass them on. I am writing to find a language and pass it on.

I am writing, writing, writing, for my life.

Think of this as a workbook.

IN THE TIME BEFORE THE MEN CAME: THE PAST AS PROLOGUE

In the time before the men came, we could do everything. We were fearless, brave, trustworthy, clean, mentally awake and morally straight.

In the time before the men came, back when we could still fly and have babies by the power of Positive Groupthink, we were Amazon women. We planned and built cities. We wrote great books and thought new thoughts and argued about ideas and aesthetics until the sun set and the moon rose and bathed us all in silver.

In the time before the men came, we were fearless, counting among our number warriors, strategists, generals and magicians who could read the tide for signs. We plotted with impunity and precision and defended our borders with a shining combination of physical strength, mental superiority and absolute courage. We had integrity, scorning the petty and the vicious, avoiding the obvious, sidestepping the curse of sloppy thinking and obsessive, possessive love that shrinks and strains and trains the ear for bickering and mediocrity as if they were the music of the spheres. We knew how to call a spade a spade.

In the time before the men came, we were bold. Explorers and wanderers, dreamers and schemers, we lived in harmony with each other and in constant search for the truth of this world and the next one. We were responsible, caring for our own and each other with a bone deep understanding of what it really means to be a part of a whole; a sister among your sisters.

In the time before the men came, we were loving, treating each other and those we trusted with a sensuality and sweetness unmatched before or since. In the time before the men came, we could still fly. *Do you remember that shit? Flying?* I mean, flying as in step-to-the-edge-of-the-mountain, bare your breasts to the North wind, rub each moon-bathed nipple three times counter-clockwise and reach out far enough and with confidence enough that from under each breast would emerge gigantic black wings with smooth blue black feathers and a span of six feet on either side. And they spread out from underneath so that we didn't fly with that difficult, upper body strength dependant motion so beloved of Icarus and the boys. We just kind of laid out on our wings and soared. The only motion necessary was a kind of rippling thing that looked the way a fish looks when it isn't in a hurry and the water is the perfect, reptilian, sub-normal degree of coolness.

And we could fly for hours without even breathing hard. In fact, we developed an entire art form based on flying. Sort of like water ballet with twelve foot wings and a touch of bop to it. That and the art of bald head painting were both lost after the men came. Two art forms that just didn't survive The Loss of Concentration...

Mythology aside, I personally was quite sorry to see bald head painting go the way of the moon worshipers and winged ballet. The intricate designs and decorations that emerged once the sisters agreed that hair was too distracting and all shaved their heads regularly were breathtaking, and since the bald head paintings were temporary, disappearing at the first serious bath or sudden rainstorm, they were all the more precious.

And even though the real radicals said they didn't see the difference between spending six hours working on cornrows and six hours working on bald head painting, most sisters were so taken with the beauty and the sensuality of the whole idea from start to finish that the movement to outlaw it quickly died and was never raised again.

But that was in the time before the men came.

See, the problem wasn't so much in their coming, but in what their coming meant to us, as Amazon women. Our magic was completely dependent on the strength of our collective concentration. Our ability to sit within the magic circle, join hands and collectively focus our minds on one thing and then achieve it. But it took the complete concentration of the entire group and so we worked hard to maintain that concentration; that focus; that power; which is one of the reasons why their lives -- why our lives -- were so peaceful. Superfluous activity is distracting. It weakens you.

So, they met twice a day in the completeness of the circle and they thought about each other and they thought about themselves and they thought about their strength and their wisdom and their passion and their lovingkindness and they thought about their power. And then they would focus intently on the pertinent question, which on any particular day might be a problem of the mind or of the heart. Reinforcement of their gifts and powers. Defense. Healing. Flying. Birth. Birth is a good example of how it worked.

In the time before the men came, we had our babies without them. What we would do when an Amazon expressed a desire to have a child, is gather in the sacred circle, in the birth configuration, say the charms for fertility and conception and then concentrate really hard. And if the time was right and the concentration was total, a girlchild would begin to grow inside her mother. Only girl children could be conjured in this way. It was, in any case, an all-female society, so the question of male children was pretty much moot.

But if the time was not right, or if the sister was not really ready, or if someone was not concentrating really hard, it didn't work and the girl baby was not conceived. In this way, the society had a kind of extrasensory method of birth control and the life of the group, it's future, was dependent on the ability of those already on the scene to concentrate and take themselves seriously. Sisterhood was in a very real sense, survival.

It was the same with flying. It only worked as a collective vision. If they all believed they could fly, they all could fly. But if one hesitated before stepping off into the freedom of, into the beauty of, the void, they were all in danger of the crash. It was necessary that close attention be paid at a serious life and death level, 24-7-365. And it was, but that was in the time before the men came.

And then one day, a young sister was hurrying back to join the midday sacred circle and she saw a man sitting outside the gates of the Amazon city. Now this was no big thing. Men lived in gender-integrated towns and villages all around the Amazons and they often had male lovers, although usually not for long. Most men grew uncomfortable trying to love a free woman over the long haul.

Amazon women didn't put much energy into the discomfort of their men friends. Discomfort was distracting. When it got to be a real problem, they simply cut their lovers loose. Their society recognized no intrinsic value in heterosexual unions and held no censure for any kind of sexual coupling that took place between consenting adults. Men, however, were not allowed to sleep within the gates of the Amazon city. Even on conjugal visits, dreaming women were considered too vulnerable to the power of the men and so at first moon, they were escorted outside the gates and wished good evening.

But somehow this man seemed different from the others she had known. It was almost as if he had a glow around his head or something. And he was holding all the things you like to see a man holding, depending on your personal preferences, style of courting and private fantasies. It could have been a dozen red roses. It could have been a first edition of Langston Hughes. It could have been a ripe watermelon or a perfect mango. It could have been a love poem. It could have been new music. It could have been his heart.

The only things it could not have been are in the category of Mercedes Benzes and Rolex watches and secure retirement plans. It has to be something that touches your soul, like it touched her soul, like it always touches mine. The real stuff. The scary stuff. The love to the grave and beyond stuff. *That's* the stuff he was holding when she saw him and it startled her and she looked into his eyes and he smiled and touched her cheek and spoke to her in a rich, chocolate brown voice full of love and sex and responsible fatherhood, and he said:

"I think you are so fine and I want to make love to you so why don't you stop doing whatever it is you're doing and come sit down here and let me rub your head and you can listen to me talk about *myself* for awhile and maybe you could tell me some things about *myself* that I hadn't thought of on my own and maybe these things will bring peace and health and prosperity to my life, and you would feel good too, when I got around to it, and hey, I think I love you."

And she was amazed to feel her knees get weak and her cheek flush crimson and, alas, she trembled and she wanted to touch him and have him touch her and she checked her watch and said to herself: "The meeting is not for fifteen minutes yet. It won't hurt to stop for just a second and see what this brother is into. Besides, I

can't see myself being swayed by a self-centered rap like that, I don't care what he's holding."
And she smiled and said: "That is the lamest rap I've heard in ages. We got cities to build, and poems to write,and gold mines to discover, and babies to create, and passion to bring into full flower. Why should I want to spend my every waking hour looking at you?"
And he said: "I don't know. Because I want you to?"
And she wanted to say: *"Nigga, pleez!"*, but she couldn't speak. She found herself paralyzed by the glow around him. She watched herself reaching up, turning her face to his, opening her lips and her arms and her softness to him and she was distracted and late and AWOL for no good reason that I can think of, can you?
And her sisters sat quietly in the circle waiting for her, couldn't start without her, powerless without her, looking at the space her presence was supposed to fill, but she didn't come and she didn't come and she didn't come, but somewhere just outside the gates of the Amazon City, she arched her back, and offered her neck and came for him / to him / with him / and her sister who was ready to begin her baby cried out and turned away and when they tried to fly away to find and save their sister, they stumbled and jumped about like crippled birds, too old, or too lame, or too silly, to take off, and it was over over, broken, finished, finito, incognito. It was once burned, twice shy and too little, too late and they staggered, powerless and broken, to the gates of the city and threw them open and saw their sister asleep and smiling, curled up on the chest of this glowing man and already forgetting the wonder of her wings, the miracle of her magic, the power of her armies.
And the man smiled when he saw them running toward their fallen sister, and tightened his arms around her and she purred in her sleep like a cream fed cat, and that was when the men came.

And the Amazons became their slaves.
And had their babies.
And cooked their dinners.
And listened to their stories.
And dreamed their dreams.
And darned their fucking socks.
And our slavery, and our powerlessness, and our fear, and our longing for the camp fires where we once held hands and sang with our sisters drove us to acts of madness and self-destruction and amnesia until we arrive at the last quarter of the twentieth century, weakened by oppression and self-hate; degraded and distracted by all the things that don't have anything to do with being a woman. An Amazon woman.

Until we arrive at the last quarter of the twentieth century straining to hear the voice of the goddess and keening in the darkness for the clarity, the serenity, the strength and the sisterhood of the time before / the time before / the time before / the men came.

MAD AT MILES

[Author's Note: This piece was developed as a performance piece and premiered at the second National Black Arts Festival in August of 1990 as part of the series "Just Us Theater Presents Live at Club Zebra!" The piece was staged with video by Zaron W. Burnett, Jr.]

I thought I wasn't going to be able to write this piece at all. I had been avoiding it for a month. Trying to think of something else to say. Something funny. After all, we are gathered here to celebrate our creative genius. Not to talk about men beating women and four a day domestic murders and all that *sexist shit*.

That wasn't the reason I almost didn't do the piece, though. I almost didn't do the piece because I thought Miles Davis had put a hex on me. I thought somehow he had found out that I was writing a piece suggesting that *he is guilty of self-confessed violent crimes against women such that we should break his albums, burn his tapes and scratch up his CD's until he acknowledges and apologizes and rethinks his position on The Woman Question.*

(That sounds terrible doesn't it? Breaking Miles Davis records? Because of a few mistakes in his personal life? Next thing you know, I'll be fussing about Two Live Crew just because they don't know the difference between rape and reciprocity...)

But I'm getting ahead of myself. I hadn't even written the piece yet. I was just thinking about it. Well, I was a little closer than that. I was sitting down to write it, but I needed to have the records. The albums in my own collection that would provide my personal connection to the subject. I needed to hear the music playing beside me in order to remember why I had been avoiding this question so energetically. And why I was so mad at Miles.

I remembered distinctly, one evening, several months ago when I was feeling particularly well organized, I pulled out the five Miles Davis records that I own and put them aside until it was time to write. But when I needed them back, I couldn't find them anywhere. I looked in all the places where they should have been. Nothing.

Finally on my third trip down to the basement for one last look, a thought popped into my mind that made my blood run cold. He knows! Miles Davis made my records disappear because somebody told him I was going to write a piece that said *he is guilty of self-confessed violent crimes against women such that we should break his albums, burn his tapes and scratch up his CD's until he acknowledges and apologizes and agrees to rethink his position on The Woman Question.*

(Didn't sound quite as bad that time, did it? The idea of it, I mean. Just the idea that we could hold a black man responsible for crimes against black women. It's still a pretty heady thought, though and not necessarily one I thought Miles would endorse, especially since he is the one I'm so mad at.)

But there's a reason for that! He's the one who admitted to it. Almost bragged about it. He's the one who confessed in print and then proudly signed his name. Nobody was ever able to show me where David Ruffin admitted to hitting Tammi Terrell in the head with a hammer, even though on the West Side of Detroit where I grew up we had all heard it from somebody who said it like they had the inside line on such things.

And nobody was able to provide me with a quote from Bill Withers describing how he beat up Denise Nicholas when their marriage was grinding to a painfully public close although people tell me JET covered the whole episode in great and gory detail.

But Miles... well, I'll let the brother speak for himself. This is an excerpt from MILES: THE AUTOBIOGRAPHY, MILES DAVIS WITH QUINCY TROUPE: *"Cecily was especially jealous of a woman taking her place in my life, but after a while she didn't have no place in my life, even though she turned down a lot of movie offers just to stay around me. Cicely's like two different women, one nice, the other one totally fucked up. For example, she used to bring her friends around anytime she wanted, but she didn't want my friends coming around. And she had some friends who I couldn't stand. One time we argued about one friend in particular, and I just slapped the shit out of her. She called the cops and went down into the basement and was hiding there. When the police came, they asked me where she was. I said, "She's around here someplace. Look down in the basement." The cop looked in the basement and came back and said, "Miles, nobody's down there but a woman, and she won't talk to me. She won't say nothing."*

So I said, "That's her, and she's doing the greatest acting job ever." Then the cop said he understood -- she

didn't look like she was hurt or nothing. I said, "Well,
she ain't hurt bad; I just slapped her once."
   The cop said, "Well, Miles, you know when we get
these calls we have to investigate."
   "Well, if she's beating my ass you gonna come with
your guns ready, too?" I asked him.
   They just laughed and left. Then I went down and
told Cicely, "I told you to tell your friend not to call over
here no more. Now if you don't tell him, I'm gonna tell
him." She ran to the phone and called him up and told
him, "Miles don't want me talking to you anymore."
Before I knew it, I had slapped her again. So she never
did pull that kind of shit on me again."

   The truth is, this is all my friend A.B.'s fault. It was
wintertime. My train got into D.C. early and I caught
the Metro out to his house. By the time I got there, there
was a fire in the fireplace, his wife Karen was up
drinking coffee and the kids were wandering around in
their nightgowns, demanding breakfast.
   Karen and A.B.'s house used to be a nun's dormitory
and they still have a built in receptacle for Holy Water in
the room where A.B. keeps his records,which is only
fitting since A.B. has the most *divine* records of anybody
I have ever known. Most of them are so rare and hard to
find that you can't even think about stealing them
because when he spots them at your house, you'd have to
say something lame and unconvincing like: "Yeah,
man, I was really lucky to find that record of the
Brazilian drummers. I know! Just like that one you
used to have before you lost it." You wouldn't have a
chance.
   And A.B. doesn't just have a lot of records, he knows
a lot about music, most especially about jazz. Which is
why I asked him to suggest something that might help
me understand about trumpets. I didn't make it any

more specific than that because it wasn't any more specific than that. I wanted to understand as much about trumpets as I had learned about saxophones from talking to A.B. about John Coltrane.

I was an innocent. He could have given me anybody. But he gave me Miles Davis. *Kind of Blue.* And he didn't even warn me that *Miles was guilty of self-confessed violent crimes against women such that we ought to break his records, burn his tapes and scratch up his CD's until he acknowledges and apologizes and agrees to rethink his position on The Woman Question.*

(It gets easier to say the more you say it. It's starting to sound almost legitimate, isn't it?)

I know I was late, the album having been recorded in March of 1959 when I was only eleven years old and if Smokey Robinson wasn't singing it, there was no way I was going to hear it, and this being the late 70's and all, but I didn't care. I was amazed by the music. I loved it, listened to it, couldn't get enough.   A.B. was pleased that his choice had been the right one and he taped the record for me before I left so I could listen to it on the train.

Which is, of course, what I did. I spent the night curled up in my tiny roomette watching America roll by outside my window and listening to Miles Davis play me into the next phase of my life.

The Bohemian Woman Phase. The single again after a decade of married phase. The last time I had a date I was eighteen and oh, god, now I'm thirty phase. The in need of a current vision of who and what and why I am phase. The cool me out quick cause I'm hanging by a thread phase.

For this frantic phase, Miles was perfect. Restrained, but hip. Passionate, but cool. He became a permanent part of the seduction ritual. Chill the wine. Light the candles. Put on a little early Miles. Give the gentleman caller an immediate understanding of what kind of woman he was dealing with. This was not a woman whose listening was confined to the vagaries of the top forty. This was a woman with the possibility of a interesting past, and the probability of an interesting future.

This was the woman I was learning to be, and I will confess that I spent many memorable evenings sending messages of great personal passion through the intricate improvisations of *Kind of Blue* when blue was the farthest thing from my mind and Miles, like I said, was perfect.

But I didn't know then that *he was guilty of self-confessed, violent crimes against women such that we ought to break his records, burn his tapes and scratch up his CD's until he acknowledges and apologizes and agrees to rethink his position on The Woman Question.*

(Still sounds pretty scary, doesn't it? Scratching up CD's and burning cassettes. Pretty right wing stuff, I know, but what are we going to do? Either we think it's a crime to hit us or we don't. Either we think our brothers have to take responsibility for stopping the war against us, or we don't.

And if we do, can we keep giving our money to Miles Davis so that he can buy a Malibu beach house and terrorize our sisters in it?

Can we make love to the rhythms of "a little early Miles" when he may have spent the morning of the day he recorded the

music slapping one of our sisters in the
mouth?
Can we continue to celebrate the genius
in the face of the monster?)

When I asked a musician friend of mine if he had
read the letter in a national magazine from a woman
who said Miles had settled out of court with her in a suit
charging him with extreme physical and mental cruelty
during the course of their lengthy professional
friendship and subsequent love affair, my friend, the
musician said, *"Is that the one he beat up at the
airport?"*
As opposed, I guess, to the one he beat up in her
apartment, or in the back seat of his limo. Or, well, you
can see how complicated the problem gets...
I tired to just forget about it. But that didn't work. I
kept thinking about Cecily Tyson hiding in the basement
of her house while the police were upstairs laughing
with Miles. I wondered what she was thinking about,
crouched down there in the darkness. I wonder if
thinking about his genius made her less frightened and
humiliated.
I wondered if his genius made it possible for her to
forgive him for _self-confessed violent crimes against
women such that we ought to break his albums, burn
his tapes and scratch his CD's until he acknowledges
and apologizes and agrees to rethink his position on The
Woman Question._

(Didn't sound bad at all that time, did it?)

I wondered if she tried to remember the last time she
had known a brother whose genius was not in the way
he played a horn, or made a living, or ran a city, but in
the way he loved her.

The danger is that we have gone so long without asking the question that we have forgotten the answer.

The danger is that we have gone so long taking what we can get that we have forgotten what we wanted.

But I can't stop thinking about it. I can't stop wondering what we would do if the violence was against black *men* instead of black *women*. Would we forgive the perpetrator so quickly and allow him into our private time; our spiritual moments; our sweet surrenders?

I can't stop wondering what our reaction would be if, say, Kenny Gee -- a resourceful, cross-over white male who is selling well enough in our community these days to tie with Anita Baker and Luther Vandross as the seduction music of choice for black urban professionals between the ages of 20 and 45...

... what if Kenny Gee was revealed to be kicking black men's asses all over the country in between concert appearances and recording sessions?

What if Kenny Gee wrote a book saying that sometimes he had to slap black men around a little just to make them cool out and leave him the fuck alone so he could get some peace and quiet?

What if Kenny Gee said this black man who saved his life and rescued his work and restored his peace of mind pissed him off so bad one day he had to slap the shit out of him? Twice.

Would Kenny Gee be the music we would play to center and calm ourselves?

Would Kenny Gee be the music we would play to relax and focus the person we love on romance?

Would Kenny Gee be the music we would play when our black male friends came to call?

And if we did and they questioned us about it -- and you know they would question us about it! -- would we explain our continuing support of Kenny Gee's music by saying: *"Yeah, I know he's beating black men and all that, but this white boy is a musical genius! I don't let personal stuff get in the way of my appreciation of his music. After all, the brothers probably asked for it. You know how it is when y'all start naggin' and shit.*"

So the question is: How can they hit us and still be our heroes?

And the question is: How can they hit us and still be our leaders? Our husbands?

Our lovers? Our geniuses? Our friends?

And the answer is...they can't.

Can they?

LAST DAY OF THE YEAR

*Is it because we bleed so regularly that everybody
thinks we are supposed to?*
Is that the reason?
Is it because they can hit us that they do hit us?

She was scrambling around in the back seat.
Terrified; clawing at the door; struggling for air in big
shuddering gasps; crying; mascara running; hair
plastered to her face; her head; her neck; the blond
highlights running with the blue shadow.
She was so wet, I thought she was raining.
I thought she was running.
I thought it was a getaway car. Like the one in
"Bonnie and Clyde" with people screaming and
hollering and second guessing every move they ever
made.
We were going to the movies. The three of us. Happy;
silly; satisfied. Rounding the corner onto I-20 with no
bigger problem than trying to decide where to eat and
what to listen to on the radio. Me and Zeke in the front
seat, feeling parental. My daughter in the back seat,
fifteen and holding.
I saw him first. Grey pants, beltless and drooping.
No shirt. No shoes. Looking for an opening between the
cars rushing onto the freeway. I thought he was a young
boy he looked so slender and gangly. Drugs, I thought.
This is some drug shit.
I hadn't seen her yet.

I think Zeke saw her first. I know he saw her before I did. I was still looking at the thin brown back of the shirtless man who was running in front of us now, hand out, eyes on fire. Zeke turned the wheel so hard I braced myself for whatever was coming next and then I saw her, off to the left, running. Screaming: "He's got a gun! He's gonna shoot me! Help me! Somebody call the police! He's trying to kill me!"

She was running toward the freeway and away from it at the same time. She was so scared, she didn't care where she was running as long as it was away from the man who was chasing her. But something in her was still frightened enough of the cars whizzing by at 70 miles an hour to hesitate, jerking her back as she tried to will her feet to risk a run into the traffic.

Zeke turned the car again, hard, and I saw the man again, right next to us. Wild-eyed, angry, distracted from the woman by the car aimed at him and gaining. He hit the car with the flat of his hand, jumping back. Zeke put the car in park, unlocked and opened the back door on the side nearest to the woman across from where my daughter sat trying to be invisible and stepped out of the car toward the man the girl was running from.

I saw him do all this as if I was looking through gauze; through rice paper; through the movie screen in silhouette. The woman was screaming.

"Get in the car," I said to her. She just kept screaming. "Get in the car," I said. "Get in the car! Get in the car!"

I could see the man over her shoulder, hurrying away, looking over his shoulder back toward us. I could feel Zeke more than I could see him. Beside my right shoulder; beyond my left arm; between the man and my daughter. In front of, and behind, and to the side of me. Everywhere and in one place. He was holding a tire iron in his right hand like it was an extension of his arm. Standing between the woman and her running man.

When the man disappeared around a hedge, she finally tumbled into the car, moaning loudly. I locked the door behind her and Zeke got back in beside me and drove smoothly onto the freeway.

The woman was hysterical. Rolling her head around; eyes squeezed tight; moans and small cries and short gasping breathes. She clawed the door like a trapped animal. My daughter's eyes were open wide and she was completely still. I looked at her and she looked back at me.

I reached for the woman's hand tossing and tensing in her lap. "You're okay," I said. "You're okay. You did the right thing. You're okay. You're okay."

I was crooning to her in what my daughter calls "the mother voice." Imminently calm. Unconditionally loving. Understanding of everything. Soothing in a way that has to do with carrying babies inside you. "You're okay," I said again. "You're okay."

She didn't believe me for a second.

"Where are we going," I said. Zeke was driving. I remember asking because I realized he was not going to the police station, even though she had said, "Call the police!" I remember hoping he wasn't going to double back and look for the guy before I remembered that this was a getaway car.

"Where, " I said, "are you driving?"

"No place," he said, very quietly. "I'm just driving."

His voice was completely neutral. He had placed the tire iron back beside the gear shift and he was looking straight ahead. The car moved as if through water. Nothing seemed to make any noise except the woman in the back, weeping and shuddering against the seat. Zeke turned on a tape: The Chambers Brothers, singing about love.

"Open your eyes," I say, still holding her hand. "Look where you are. You're okay. You're okay." I thought she was going to jump out of the car. Too afraid to sit still for too long. "You're okay," I say again. "You're okay." She looks at me straight for the first time. "Where do you want us to take you," I say. My timing is off. I made the request too soon. Her eyes panic. "I,I..." she is trying to tell me something. "I have asthma," she says, still gasping. "It's okay, " I say. "Just relax. Take your time."

She is still holding my hand, but I don't think she knows it. She looks very young. Less than twenty. I could be her mother.

There is a lot of make-up smeared on her face. Tears and snot are everywhere. I hand her a Kleenex and she mops at her face and gulps air, trying to regulate her breathing. She looks at me again and then away.

"Thank you," she says. "Thank you for stopping." She speaks to me, but she means all of us. I nod. Zeke is still driving. She gives me an address not far from where we are. We know exactly where it is. She lives less than three blocks from the house I used to live in with my daughter's father. In the neighborhood.

She asks to be let off on the other side of the street and lets my hand go without the sisterly squeeze I wanted for my own reassurance that she was okay. Safe. That someone strong and brave and loving was waiting for her on the other side of that door.

She was really small. High-heeled, thigh-high boots. Skin-tight jeans. Clutching her purse and an old brown sweater. She walked with the mincing little off-balance steps that high-heeled shoes demand and I tried to imagine her running down I-20 in those shoes.

She vomited just outside her apartment door and disappeared inside.

And how can they prey on us and save us, all at the same time?

And how can they possess us and abandon us all at the same time?

And how can we tell the villains from the heroes and the beaters from the leaders and the good guys from the bad guys?

By what they *do*, not what they *say*.

By whether they stop to help, or just drive on.

By whether they are prepared not just to *accept* our anger, but to *share* it and *spare* it and save us from themselves and their brothers gone mad, or *driven* mad, but either way, too mad to figure out how to be with us.

Later, when I kissed my daughter good-night, she said, "I am scared to go to sleep. I think something bad is going to happen."

And I kissed her again and assured her in the mothervoice that it was the events of the day that were scaring her. That she was safe here in a house with people who loved her and would protect her and *could* protect her and she didn't need to worry. And she believed me. Because it was true.

So far, so good...

THE OTHER FACTS OF LIFE

These are the other facts of life. The ones your mother probably didn't tell you because she didn't want to scare you. What she didn't realize was that being scared isn't the most terrible thing that can happen. *Being unprepared is much worse.*

Violence:
In America, they *admit* that five women a day are killed by their husbands, boyfriends, ex-husbands, ex-boyfriends or lovers. That doesn't count the women killed during random rapes, murders, robberies and kidnappings.

In America, the main reason women are ever hospitalized is because they've been beaten and tortured by men. More than for childbirth. More than for cancer care. More than from heart attacks.

In America, thousands of women a day are raped and/or tortured and abused by men in as many ways as you can think of, and probably a whole lot more you haven't thought of, and don't want to, including beating, shooting, scalding, stabbing, slapping, shaking and starving.

The facts indicate that we are under siege, incredibly vulnerable, totally unprepared and *too busy denying the truth to collectively figure out what to do about it.* Men beat and torment and rape women because they *can.* They're usually bigger and physically stronger and they've structured a culture that condones absolutely the possession and control of women by any means necessary. All this puts us at a tremendous disadvantage, especially since our group is usually fragmented and disorganized. We can't depend on each other for protection yet, and won't be able to until we admit to the problem and then learn something about self defense. Until that happens, individual knowledge of how to recognize and get out of dangerous situations is crucial to our survival.

All men are *capable* of abusing women, no matter what they tell you or what they call it, so don't kid yourself about this one or that one being different. It takes *years* of love, work and trust to eliminate the probability of violence in relationships between men and women. *Don't think you can rush the process because you wish you could.*

Don't trust *any* male strangers. They are guilty until proven innocent. Don't accept rides, favors, gifts, free advice, or compliments from men you don't know. Strangers are always dangerous and friends can be, too, when they are angry, frustrated, confused or crazed by a sexist desire for possession and control of you. [The section on "BASIC TRAINING" has a working definition of the word "sexist" if you don't already have one.]

Learn to recognize these ten early warning signals as a way of *anticipating* violence in order to *avoid* it if at all possible:

1. shouting, hollering, excessive cursing, name calling, sarcasm;

2. finger pointing or fist waving, especially in and around your face;

3. arm or wrist grabbing or twisting.

4. throwing or breaking things;

5. hitting his head or his fist against walls, tables, steering wheel, etc. or reckless fast driving;
6. threatening to do violent things to himself, you, your family, your friends, your children;
7. indicating that he has a gun or other weapon;
8. bringing up past arguments or wrongdoing for which he holds you responsible;
9. following you, spying on you, questioning you about your whereabouts or your friends, male or female;
10. locking doors so you are trapped in a car or house and can't leave whenever you want to leave. If any of these signals occur, stay focused and alert. Do whatever you can to diffuse the situation (short of having a sexual exchange which is rape) and leave by yourself as soon as possible. Always have cab fare / bus fare / train fare and change for the telephone in your purse. Your life may depend on it.

If this happens in your own house, you should still leave until you can be safe there. Take your children if you can. Go to a friend or a relative. Go to the police station. Go to a fire station (there will always be someone there awake and on duty). Go to a hotel and call for help from the lobby. Tell somebody you need help until you get it.

Violence is never justified. It should *never* be forgiven. Apologies and pleas for forgiveness should fall on deaf ears. If a man beats you / hits you / shoves you / slaps you / torments you once, *he will do it again.* Cut him loose.

Rape:
Review the facts at the start of the last section on violence. Let yourself think about them and feel what they really mean to each of us. Keep them in mind while you think about rape.

Rape is a crime of womanhating and violence. It is *not* a crime of passion or a sex crime.

The victim of rape is *never, never, never* responsible, no matter what she was wearing, where she was walking, what she was doing or who she went out with, had a drink with, married, kissed, flirted with or lied to. Bad judgment and carelessness are not punishable by rape.

No rape is ever justified and no rapist has an acceptable reason or excuse. *Ever.*

To protect yourself against being raped by strangers:

1.   Secure the place you live with your choice of burglar bars, alarms, dogs, alert neighbors, good lighting and/or a gun you are licensed and trained to use.

2.   *Always* lock your car doors and be alert to men on the street when you stop at intersections.

3.   Learn to change a tire quickly. Practice doing it in the dark. Don't run out of gas.

4.   Try to wait for the bus with a friend or neighbor or co-worker especially at night. Avoid waiting or getting off at places where groups of men gather. (Bars, labor pools, shelters, liquor stores, basketball courts, pool halls, etc.)

5.   Try not to walk alone at night, but if you have to, walk in the middle of the street so you are in the light and away from the bushes and alleys. Keep your hands free and carry mace.

6.   Check for men lurking in underground parking lots, empty buildings and vacant lots.

7.   Don't ever accept rides with strangers or men you don't know well enough to trust *absolutely*.

8.   Be conscious of the kinds of clothes that men say make them think we want to be raped by them. These include tight pants and sweaters, very high heeled shoes, short skirts, halter tops, see-through clothes, etc.

9. Stay in shape so you can run if you need to run.
10. Practice hollering as loud as you can so you can make a big noise if you are attacked.

To protect yourself from being raped by men you know:

1. Never be alone with a man you don't know well and trust *absolutely*. This takes time. Trust your instincts. Take responsibility for setting the pace and structure of the relationship. Remember the violence warning signals.

2. Don't park or drive in isolated places with men you don't know well and trust absolutely. Whenever possible, take your own car on first dates and drive it yourself.

3. Don't flirt or accept flirting behavior if you're not interested in having sex within the next few hours.

4. Don't go to apartments, houses or hotels with men you don't know well and trust absolutely.

5. Scream and fight back when the first unwelcome sexual approach is made and you realize what is happening. Trust your instincts. *If you think it's happening, it is happening.* Don't wait to protest. Holler. Loud. A "friend" or "date" is not likely to want your noise to draw neighbors, family, friends, police, etc.

6. Don't go out alone with groups of men that you don't know well and trust absolutely. Evaluate each member of the group individually. The men you know well should always outnumber the men you don't know well. Ask *yourself* why there are no other women there. Ask *them* the same question.

7. Don't watch highly sexual movies, read sexually exciting books or magazines, or talk and tease about sexual things with a man you don't intend to have sex with in the next few hours.

8. Don't kiss and hug and fondle a man you don't intend to have sex with in the next few hours.

9. Don't drink, get high or fall asleep around men you don't know well and trust absolutely.
10. Don't allow any physical contact that you do not initiate, appreciate and fully endorse.

If you are as careful as you can be and you are still attacked and/or raped, *don't panic*. Stay alert. Focus on staying alive and unhurt. Try to remember everything you can about the rapist, the location, the circumstances. As soon as you can, get to safety. Call the police. Call a woman friend to come and be with you. Call your doctor. Call the rape crisis center.

Remember that you are the *victim* and don't take any shit from anybody.

Sex:

Sex is a powerful and basic drive meant to insure the survival of the species. In order to help insure that we Do It, sex can also be pleasurable when it is a voluntary exchange between equals. But sex is not exempt from the madness that is everywhere between men and women. In fact, sex is usually the most volatile and misunderstood battleground of all.

Remember when you think about sex that men often use it to express power, control, womanhating and violence. Phrases like *"I knocked the bottom out of it,"* and *"I fucked her brains out"* are the norm, not the exception. Even worse, sex and female sexuality have been tainted, consciously or unconsciously, by male misinterpretation.

Don't be fooled into imitating what you see in the movies, on t.v. or read in the books that crowd the best-seller lists. Trust yourself. Learn your body. Listen to it. Touch it. Figure out what feels good and what doesn't. Don't confuse pain and pleasure. If it's hurting you, it shouldn't be pleasing him.

Take *complete responsibility* for birth control. Of course, in the best of all possible worlds, men would share equal responsibility for birth control, but realistically speaking, they won't take it as seriously as we do. They can't get pregnant.

Take *complete responsibility* for safe sex. Protect yourself against AIDS and other sexually transmitted diseases by always carrying and using your own condoms.

Don't fake pleasure, excitement or orgasms. There is no excuse for it, no end to it, and no way to justify it. Whenever you find yourself considering "faking it", ask yourself why and who benefits from such bullshit?

Most of the ways people get together sexually fall into three categories: *mating, making love and having sex.*

Mating is the conscious coupling of two people with the agreed upon intention to have a child. It is the only kind of sexual exchange that can only occur between heterosexuals. "Agreed upon" is the key phrase here. If both people don't agree, the energy won't be in sync and the kid will suffer for it. Also, tricking somebody into bearing or fathering a child when they haven't agreed to it is low down and unfair.

Making Love is communicating sexually on a high physical, mental, emotional and spiritual plane with someone you know, respect, love, trust and desire passionately. Hold out for this kind of sex if you can. Although it is almost impossible to achieve in the midst of the current crisis, it is worth the wait.

Having sex is the catch all description of all the other sexual exchanges that occur and it has several sub-categories.

1. *Lustful sex* -- this is a purely physical response to another person. Nothing wrong with it. Be careful about safe sex and birth control. Lust cares nothing for public health questions so plan ahead and come

prepared. Lust also gets careless about safety, so review the sections on Rape and Violence.

2. *Sympathy sex* -- nothing wrong with this either, except it is often misinterpreted. If the person is so depressed or distraught or disillusioned that sex is the only way you can think of to cheer him/her up (this is *your* idea, right?) then this person is probably in serious need of an anchor, an angel, a savior. What was meant to be simple sympathy sex often ends up with messy misunderstandings on both sides. Avoid it if possible and take your friend out for a cup of cappucino instead.

3. *Angry sex* -- a commonly made mistake, especially in long-term relationships where there isn't enough breathing and pacing room. Don't do it. This kind of sex encourages you to use your sexuality in a way that ultimately denies you pleasure and twists your spirit. This kind of sex may also trigger male violence and female depression. *Don't do it.*

4. *Friendship sex* -- this can be alright, but it must be controlled by you absolutely. There is a tendency for men who like you to become possessive and controlling once you begin to have friendship sex. Don't act like it's cute when it happens and don't indulge or reward it with more sex. If you value the friendship and you see this happening, stop all sexual activity immediately. Explain why and be unshakable in your decision not to resume sexual relations. Good friends are hard to find.

BASIC TRAINING: THE BEGINNINGS OF WISDOM

"*Woman*," Japanese feminist/artist Yoko Ono once said, "*is the nigger of the world.*"
I have always found that quote from Yoko offensively interesting. Who was she talking to? The question assumes one cannot be a female and a "nigger" at the same time. Where does that leave black women? Maybe that makes us the *nigger-nigger* of the world. Double niggers. The mind boggles at the kind of oppression that would await such a cursed being. A creature oppressed by racism and sexism, buffeted from niggerhaters to womanhaters and back again with hardly time enough to take a deep breath and try to figure out what to do about it. And to make matters worse, the poor doomed thing lives in America. I would suspect even Yoko Ono's fertile imagination could not conceive of such a fate.
I know the feeling. Last summer, I opened the morning newspaper to read that a twelve year old black girl had been discovered last evening by her mother, lying dead in the middle of the living room floor, her face beaten to a bloody pulp, her jump rope tied around her neck and a broom handle rammed up into her vagina. The crime took place during daylight hours in a heavily trafficked area of a crowded apartment complex, but nobody saw anything or anybody unusual. As I write these words, almost a year later, the murderer is still at large.
When I read that story, the first thing I felt was fear. Had things gotten so bad that the fiend who was capable of committing such a crime could blend into our

neighborhoods without causing a ripple? The thought was chilling, especially since the summer had been filled with news reports of an escalating wave of black male violence directed primarily toward black women and children on the streets, in their cars, in their own homes.

A series of murders of elderly black women raped and strangled in their beds. A black mother kidnapped at the bus stop and sodomized on the nearby railroad tracks in full view of her screaming baby daughter. Black women snatched off the street by a rapist who gouges out their right eyes to subdue them. Ex-wives and estranged lovers stalked and shot down outside their jobs by the men they used to sleep with. And now this last one, too horrible to be ignored or explained away, no matter how they tried to sanitize it for the six o'clock news.

I had never felt quite so frightened; quite so helpless; quite so *angry*. But angry at who and for what and in what context? As if on cue, the chorus of smoothly cautionary black male voices that lives inside my head spoke as one.

Surely I couldn't condemn *all* black men for the murderous violence of a few "bad apples." Surely I wouldn't be so hysterical as to label *all* black men dangerous because there were some criminals among their number. Surely I understood the danger and divisiveness of perpetrating such "negative images" of black men. Surely I wasn't so ignorant of our history as to decry the horror of these crimes without placing the ultimate blame where it belonged, on white racism and the unfocused, but *understandable* anger it produces in black men. Surely I am clear that it is not "the brothers" who are the problem. It's "the Man." Right?

Wrong. It's The Brothers. Period. Although all African American insanity, male and female, can ultimately be explained by the long ago presence of the slave ships pulling up on the coast of Africa, that blood soaked presence cannot continue to be an acceptable reason for our current sorry state. We cannot undo slavery. It happened. We cannot ignore racism. It is a fact of our lives. But we *can* begin to work on the ways that racism makes us turn on each other. Black men must begin to take *personal responsibility* for the way they treat us and the way they treat our children.

There is no white man physically present in the house when a black man decides to beat his wife. There is no white man present when black men prey on women old enough to be their grandmothers to get money for crack. There is no white man present when black girls are not safe from rape in their own neighborhoods or in their own front rooms. There is no white man present at the conception of a black baby, who will be born with AIDS because the father has been sharing needles.

And, *yes*, I really do understand that white men are responsible for the madness, but who is responsible for the cure?

I also understand that racism is a heavy burden to bear and can make black men feel mean and hostile and crazy because it makes black women feel crazy too.

And I understand that white men are hard to work for, hard to live around, hard to pass on the street and hard to figure out a way around because all that is hard for black women, too.

And I understand the danger of being black in America where white men control the guns because that is dangerous for black women, too.

I understand the frustration of last hired, first fired because black women are the only group in the nation with worse employment statistics than black men in *every* category and at *every* wage level. (Bitter, unprovable -by -any- statistics -anywhere accusations by brothers who tell us that being black and female gives us an unfair advantage in the marketplace notwithstanding.)

I understand the horror of poor health care and its attendant ills because black women have the worst health profile of any group in the United States. I understand it's hard trying to make ends meet, get ahead in the world, be a good person, find time for yourself, love your children, and be active in your community because we have a hard time with all that too.

I understand and experience all the dangers and frustrations and limitations of being black in America because I am black in America. Black *and* female. Being black and male isn't any worse. It's just *different.* Brothers who try to make a case for black men suffering more keenly from the effects of racism than black women are either lying or misinformed.

Besides, it is a no-win competition. They get shot more; we get raped regularly. They do more heroin; we're into crack. We're *all* in terrible shape because of the presence of racism and sexism in our lives. Debate about who is the most victimized victim doesn't take us anywhere but deeper into victimhood and is usually a smoke screen thrown up by brothers in an effort to keep the discussion focused on *race* and not on *gender.*

Sexism is still not a word that gets used much in the black community, even though it describes a form of oppression that effects the majority population of the community -- women!-- and is no less virulent and deadly than racism. This other "ism" is real, present and provable, just like racism. It oppresses black women with depressing and dependable regularity, just like racism, and it has been thoroughly documented as a fact of American life. Just like racism.

In spite of this overload of available information, most black men won't even admit to the existence of sexism, certainly not within their own communities and almost never in their own lives. They won't entertain serious discussion of it or accept it as a fact of life within every black household in the country.

The fact that black men routinely and cavalierly deny something that is a critical element in our African American female reality makes us feel crazy since it seems so clear to us we don't understand why *they* can't see it. It also robs us of the possibility of working cooperatively with our brothers on defining the problem and trying to solve it. If black men won't admit that their sexism and male chauvinism and domestic violence are problems, how can we consider them allies in the search for creative solutions?

We can't. Not yet. Not until they are willing to redefine their black male reality to incorporate the equally valid reality of our black female experiences. Not until they are prepared to recognize and admit to their role as oppressors in the struggle against sexism and see their crimes as no less serious than the crimes committed in defense of racism.

This is a difficult process, made no less difficult by the fact that we, black women, have no adequate language with which to *describe* our situation, to ourselves or to anyone else. Most of us have accepted black men's indifference to or hostility toward sexism as good enough reasons to ignore the problem. We therefore don't even have working definitions of the words needed to begin to articulate our specific black female reality.

Our history of thinking about struggle is so shaped by our experiences with white American racism that when we begin to talk about oppression we invariably get sidetracked into talking about racism *only*. We are, of course, encouraged in this by The Brothers, who much prefer the more familiar and acceptable status of oppressed victim to the less admiral role of the violent oppressor.

As a result of this absence of regular, widely accessible discussion on the subject of sexism and how it messes up our lives, many intelligent, aware, politically conscious black men and women go through those lives with no working definitions of the basic concepts which establish the context for any serious struggle against sexism; no continuing dialogue with each other about that struggle; and no mutually accepted standard against which to evaluate their own behavior and the behavior of others. In the swirl of our collective ignorance, no clarity is possible, no dialogue productive, and the problem goes undefined.

An old Chinese proverb says that the beginning of wisdom is to call all things by their proper names. The process of naming and defining begins the process of discovery. It is in that spirit that I offer Basic Training.

Basic Training is useful for personal discovery or review, helpful in discussions with your sisters and *critical* to the creative enlightenment of The Brothers. No black woman should attempt to discuss anything about sexism with a black man before he has mastered the basics. Such a discussion is doomed to failure and holds the potential for sparking anger and non-productive exchanges.

Moreover, any black man who will not take the time to master Basic Training isn't being serious about a question we've already said is life and death to us and he doesn't deserve your time, your attention and your lovingkindness.

The following ten basic definitions, concepts and approaches together make up Basic Training. Here they are:

1.   *Sexism* -- all the ways men mess over women from the cradle to the grave and which are painfully evident in all rituals, institutions, educational systems, cultural expressions, family structures, religions and economic systems that men have devised; a social, economic, political, spiritual or sexual relationship in which males have authority over females based solely on gender.

It is *impossible* to live in America and not be tainted by sexism *and* a participant in it, either as a victim or a perpetrator. As women, by the end of our African American girlhoods, we have learned and perfected a dizzying variety of slave behaviors which we are rewarded for mastering by the men who made them up in the first place.

As men, they were taught that we were inferior, unworthy of their respect, subject to their whim and present on earth primarily for their sexual pleasure and the bearing and mothering of their children.

We were *all* taught that it is acceptable for them to hit us when they think we have "asked for it" and that their opinions carry more weight in all critical decisions simply because they were men and therefore assumed to be of superior knowledge and more vast experience.

2.   *Sexist* -- a person who practices *sexism*, consciously or unconsciously, by living in a way that endorses, perpetuates, and prolongs it. *All* men-- including black men -- born and raised in America are sexists, even those who are consciously struggling against it. Men are never completely cured of sexism. They can, however, consciously and consistently alter their behavior. Sort of like recovering alcoholics.

An integral part of that recovery process is the admission of culpability, responsibility and the element of choice. Ignorance of the problem, feigned or real, is no excuse for inaction. Men run the world. The fact that they are oppressing women can't have just slipped by them. The means to stop the problem are within their control. If they don't do it, it's because they don't *want* to do it.

Black men, because they are oppressed and influenced by white men often express their sexism is ways identical to the ways the white men they so despise express racism. The irony of this is usually lost on black men, but should make it clear to us that there is a big difference between clarity on *race* and clarity on *sexism*. The two are definitely related and usually complimentary, but absolutely *not* interchangeable.

3. *Feminism* -- the belief that women are full human beings capable of participation and leadership in the full range of human activities -- intellectual, political, social, sexual, spiritual and economic. Feminism is to sexism what black nationalism is to racism; the most rational response to the problem.

4. *Feminist* -- a woman who believes in and practices *feminism* in working to eliminate her own internalized sexism and the sexism of those around her. Although men are allowed to call themselves *feminists* in some liberal feminist circles, I do not endorse this practice. Men can be enlightened, but I have never met a man who did not cling to and exemplify sexist behavior from time to time in spite of himself. Letting them dub themselves *feminists* tends to lead to smugness, self-satisfaction and the feeling that the man who is struggling to overcome his own sexism and the sexism of his brothers has somehow achieved a more exalted status, a safe conduct pass that allows him to be a little less rigorous on himself, having demonstrated his good intentions. I am reminded of my grandmother's admonition about what paves the road to hell.

5. *Racist* is to black people what *Sexist* is to women; The Enemy. Race plays a major role in our perceptions

about sexism, our strategies for fighting against it, and black men's primarily unenlightened responses to, examinations of, the question, especially those that include discussion of their own sexist behavior. Racism adds a layer of anger and stress in our lives as black people that makes it even more difficult for us to take on the responsibility of fighting yet another deadly "ism". Struggling against sexism as part of a group that is also racially oppressed is like walking to work with bad feet: you know you have to do it, but those bunions make the journey just that much harder.

But in trying to talk to black men about sexism (or to understand it more clearly ourselves) our racial history is an invaluable tool. Black men who have experienced racism are already familiar with what oppression *looks* like, how it *operates*, how it can permeate and poison every area of your life. The problem is, we have not figured out a way to use that racial knowledge to help them understand sexism and their role in it.

Let me explain. By the time I was eight or nine, I understood clearly that slavery and racism had created a complex set of circumstances that impacted daily on my life as an African American. Factors such as where I lived, how I lived, what jobs I could get, how clean the grocery stores were in my neighborhood, the probability that I'd get robbed and raped were all in some way circumscribed by the presence of white racism.

I also knew that as a person who had the advantage of growing up in a house where there were books, it was my responsibility once I achieved adulthood to work consciously to "uplift the race", or at least as much of it as I could, given limited resources, human frailty and the awesome implacability of the group itself.

I also had a world view though which to filter the complex racial stimuli that I was receiving from books, from teachers and from the media. I knew that every aberrant form of African American behavior could be understood -- not *justified* but completely understood -- by admitting to the reality of the slave ship; to the raping of wives in front of their husbands; to the selling of babies torn from their mother's arms. My family made it clear to me that there was no way we as a people could recover from such barbarism and injustice in less than 200 years. Complete clarity on that basic point was necessary to establish a context for understanding why black folks do the things we do and being able to love us anyway.

I also had another invaluable tool for understanding my position as an oppressed African American -- *a definable adversary*. White racism, represented and perpetrated by white people, through a maze of institutions, laws and customs they are prepared to defend with their lives, and whenever possible *our* lives, was that adversary. I understood that white people had been raised by their culture to be racist in order to maintain status and control and I was encouraged to question everything they did or said since it was never going to be in my best interest to believe them without checking some reliable black source first, preferably my family since they had a vested interest in my not acting a fool.

All this critical information and racial analysis were presented to me as an integral part of my daily life, not a special ceremony during black history month. These African American survival lessons were part of the fabric of family; expected, accepted and continuous.

A good example of this routine is the running commentary my politically radical and highly opinionated family would offer during the nightly news. I grew up, in fact, hearing two news casts. The one the white male t.v. newscaster (they were all white males back then) was giving and the one my family was giving in a kind of sepia toned simulcast.

When the newsguy said something critical about Patrice Lumumba, my mother reminded him that the Belgians used to cut off the hands of captured Africans in order to terrorize them into being slaves. When the guy said something sketchy about the reasons for a recent violent crime wave in the black community, my stepfather filled in the missing pieces and then wondered aloud who had put this fool on the air anyway.

In this way, I learned early to have no respect for what white men said about being black, and, by extension, about anything else. This self-confidence and clarity grew directly out of my racial self-awareness and gave me a powerful tool for understanding the seemingly random and increasingly frightening events of the sixties. I had an oppressed person's most potent weapons: information, analysis and positive group identity.

As I began to seriously understand what it meant to be black *and* female in America, the tools my family gave me for the development of a black consciousness were, and are, invaluable. But how do we transfer racial understanding to a discussion of sexism? What is the process by which we can use what we know about being *black* to understand and articulate what we know about being black *women?*

The next three basics should help us begin that delicate process.

6. *Racism* and *sexism* are systems of oppression designed to control, confine and exploit one group of people (the *oppressed)* for the benefit of another group of people (the *oppressor*). In discussions of *racism*, black people are the oppressed and white people are the oppressors. In our discussions of *sexism*, black women are the oppressed and black men are the oppressors.

7. *Sexism* operates a lot like *racism* except it is based on *sexual* identity instead of *racial* identity. Women of *all* social and economic classes are oppressed by sexism.

8. In discussions of *race* between black people and white people, the conscious black person is *always* right; is always the ultimate authority on questions having to do with race and racism; must *always* be regarded as the "injured party," or the oppressed. The reason for this is obvious. It is in the best interest of white people to keep black people oppressed. They cannot possibly be expected to be objective about questions of race and should therefore adopt a *listening*, not a speaking posture.

9. In discussions of *sexism*, the conscious woman is *always* right; *always* the ultimate authority on questions having to do with sexism; *always* the "injured party," or oppressed. The reasons for this are obvious. It is in men's best interest to keep women oppressed and under their control. They cannot be expected to be objective -- no matter how loudly and self-righteously they protest -- about questions of sexism and should therefore adopt a *listening* rather than a speaking posture.

This last Basic may be the most difficult of all for black men to deal with. The idea of agreeing in *advance* that a black woman will be the ultimate and final authority on all questions regarding any subject is inconceivable to most black men. They are convinced they know more than we do about everything -- *even about us!*-- and most black men will argue and pout and rant and rave about how stupid, unfair, unacceptable and unenlightened such a condition is. Let him vent for an appropriate but not self-indulgent amount of time and then ask him how many times he has let a white man tell him *anything* about what it feels like to be a black man. If he hesitates, refer him back to Basic numbers seven and eight.

See what I mean about how helpful the racial comparisons can be?

One cautionary note. Honest discussions of sexism are always emotionally intense no matter what the sex of the participants. Exchanges between men and women on sexism and related topics are especially charged. Understanding this reality, it is important to establish that in addition to always being *right,* the black women involved in such discussions have the right to establish the acceptable vocabulary and appropriate level of emotional and physical response in *any and all* discussions with The Brothers about matters regarding any aspect of sexism.

So, last but not least, Basic number 10:

10. No hollering, waving of arms or objects in a threatening or excited manner, cursing and name calling during discussions of sexism and sexist behavior without explicit permission from the Sister in control, as in this exchange:

Brother says: " May I throw this tape player across the room in your direction to show my anger at your defining me as a sexist and perhaps intimidate you into being quiet by introducing the possibility of violence into this exchange?"

Sister says: " No, and please stop pounding your fist against the wall while we talk."

The reason, again, is obvious. Domestic violence is the front lines of the war against women. Black men, consciously and unconsciously, use the threat of violence, the fact of their superior strength and their well known volatility to keep black women nervous and frightened. A man who will holler and throw things at you or around you when there is a disagreement has already introduced violence into the environment. He will probably also feel that he can grab you, push you, or shake his fingers or fist in your face. *This is dangerous, oppressive, sexist behavior.* Ask him to stop, explaining why if you can. If he doesn't stop, or becomes more threatening or exasperated or coldly sarcastic, end the discussion as neutrally as possible and then find some quiet time alone to evaluate the brother's actions and your appropriate response.

It is important to remember that men beat and kill women *regularly*. The threat and the *actuality* of violence are the keys to male domination and control of women. Most black men, having been raised in a sexist country, have at some level absorbed the acceptability of violence against women. Be alert. Take responsibility for monitoring the emotional level of the discussions and controlling it. It is our *safety* and well being that are at stake.

If your efforts at discussing these questions honestly continue to degenerate into emotionally or potentially physically violent episodes, ask yourself why you continue to try to have the discussion with someone who isn't interested. Give yourself an honest answer and then decide how to proceed.

One final note. During the discussions that will accompany mastering the Basics, some brothers may attempt to speak to you in what I have named *mantones*. This is the tone of voice regularly used by men to address women and children and other perceived inferiors.

Other distinguishing features of the mantone are the assumption of all available authority and an unshakeable belief in the superiority of male intellect and moral fiber. A *mantone* is always condescending, often sarcastic and has been known to reduce grown women to weeping and cursing wrecks with its implacable certainty and smug inability to *listen* to anything a woman has to say.

Mantones are by their very nature and intent oppressive, sexist, *learned* behavior. They can be *unlearned* once they are agreed to be mutually unacceptable behavior.

Most women are aware of *mantones* although we have not had a word to describe them clearly, making it impossible to get any agreement on outlawing them. The Brothers may have a difficult time understanding the concept of *mantones*, but once you have had the initial discussion, you can begin to point the tones out to him whenever they occur -- in him, in the media, in his friends, etc. Simply reference your initial discussion and point out the example. As in: "Remember the other day when we were talking about *mantones*? Well, this is one."

Examples will be *everywhere* and as he begins to understand the whole idea and hear the arrogance and obnoxiousness of *mantones* for himself, a brother of good heart will begin to work seriously to eliminate his own *mantones* as quickly as possible.

It will be helpful to review Basic number nine before beginning the discussion of *mantones* to eliminate unnecessary objections to the obvious.

IN MY SOLITUDE

I have been in love continuously since I was 6 years old. When I was in first grade, the 7-year-old object of my affections had just moved to Detroit from Montgomery, Alabama. His wonderfully old-fashioned name was Turner Crooks. Now, maybe it was his shy southernness, in such sweet contrast to the more direct Detroit styles of my other classmates. Or maybe it was his closely cropped hair with the perfect part cut delicately into the left side. Or maybe it was the starched plaid shirts his mother sent him to school in every day. Or it might even have been something as mundane as the fact that "Crooks" followed "Cleage" in our alphabetized class roll, so Turner spent a good six hours of each day literally breathing down my neck. Whatever it was, he made my heart skip, my cheeks flush crimson and, for some inexplicable reason, my toes turn in.

But that's not this story. This is a story about the years between ages 6 and 30, when I spent a good portion of my every waking hour thinking obsessively and lovingly about one male or another. This is a story about that moment of realization that comes when you add up all the hours of your life and realize that you haven't allocated any time for your *self*. I realized this surprising fact when I was looking closely at how I spent my time, in the hope of squeezing out more of it to write (my passion and my livelihood). It seemed that I never had enough, and I couldn't figure out why. So I tried to examine my day and came up with the following percentages: Friends, 5; Family, 5; Child, 15; Work, 15; Maintenance, 10; Lover, 50.

I was appalled. As I looked at my list and tried to understand what it meant, I realized that there was no category for *"Self."* I had completely abandoned any organized attempts to spend time alone, enjoying and developing my own company, in favor of spending as much time as possible with the man who was closest to me. I had to admit that all the time I didn't spend working or raising my daughter or paying the gas bill was being gratefully, happily, excitedly given away to the men I loved.

I told myself that it wasn't true, that I was a conscious feminist who would never fall into such a trap. I told myself that I wasn't one of those women who becomes so man-centered that she blurs the line between herself and himself.

But is that all bad? I argued back to myself. A truly loving, liberated relationship is healthy, life-affirming, mutually beneficial and empowering to both parties. I reminded myself that my current relationships with men were (after many years of struggle) sane, affectionate, intelligent and supportive. I told myself that I could be alone whenever I wanted to, but that I didn't want to. I didn't need to. I've had enough time alone, I said to myself. Then another voice inside my head asked gently: When did you have enough? Which is when I realized that ever since I turned six and fell in love with Turner Crooks, the pride of Montgomery, Alabama, I had had almost none.

Starting with that first fall, I'd been in love and attentive in a way that had given me the ability to understand, interpret and appreciate the nuances of Black male behavior in a way that delighted and inspired my men friends. Their reactions, in turn, rewarded and reaffirmed my worth in this distressingly male-dominated culture and convinced me, at a subconscious level, that listening to and understanding them was a far more critical and worthwhile undertaking than applying the same unblinking eye, attentive ear and generous heart to my own womanhood. But the question was, if I was looking at *them* and they were looking at *them*, who was looking at *me*?

As I thought about all of this, I realized that there were a number of things that were important to my inner strength and peace that I didn't do much of anymore. I listed ten right off the top of my head:

Things I Do Only When I'm Alone: (1) Write; (2) Listen to my Smokey Robinson records; (3) Buy flowers; (4) Make photo collages; (5) Think in the shower (or dream in the bathtub); (6) Read; (7) Sing; (8) Swim; (9) Meditate; (10) Plan ahead.

I was uncomfortably surprised by how many of these things that nurtured my creative life had been abandoned. I also realized that I had indulged in many of them only during the brief period following my divorce when I was too busy healing my emotional wounds to fall obsessively in love. I realized that I would have to validate the whole idea of solitude by choice and then figure out how to structure it. It was harder than I realized.

I was up against a culture that tells you the highest good is to find a man and spend every minute with him. I was up against women friends who say that letting a good man roam the Atlanta streets unattended, even for a few hours of solitude, is like dropping a lamb into a lion's den. I faced the insecurities that are the special purview of women turning 40. I was up against the guilt of not giving a lover my time and focus whenever he wanted them, a habit learned with the lesson of how to make conversation about sports. And, most persuasively, I was up against the sweet weapons at the disposal of loving Black men who want to have your undivided attention. I feared that choosing to spend time regularly with myself was tantamount to taking a secret lover with unfamiliar habits and priorities. What was solitude anyway, I asked myself, and how was I supposed to get it? I decided to begin at the beginning.

One of my earliest memories is coming home from school to find my mother seated at the piano playing *"Solitude"*, the Duke Ellington classic that Billie Holiday made her own. Now, my mother often played the piano and sang, but not like this. On these occasions she became somebody else entirely. She would close her eyes, throw back her head and sing with a fierce intensity and longing that I was still too young to understand.

She would still be wearing the same neat dress and sensible shoes she'd been teaching school in all day, as if it would take too long to change into more comfortable clothes. If she had stopped at the store, there would be grocery bags tossed on the kitchen table; ice cream and frozen orange juice being, at that moment, beside the point.

Although at that time my sister and I weren't really sure what the point was, we had sense enough to know that we should stay out of sight and sound until the moment passed. When my mother finished the song, she would sit quietly at the piano for a few minutes and then hang her coat in the living-room closet, and start on dinner.

My parents had been divorced less than a year at that time, and my personal theory concerning these passionate piano solos was that my mother secretly longed for a reconciliation with my father. When I asked her to confirm this theory years later, she laughed and shook her head. "Reconciliation? I was looking for someplace quiet to collect my thoughts," she said. "*That's* the solitude I was talking about!"

Solitude. Even the word sounds old-fashioned and wistful. It conjures up visions of large, empty rooms and lonely, reclusive people. Hardly a state anyone would yearn to be in, but hardly a definition that applies to solitude either. Loneliness is to solitude what a beat-up old Volkswagen is to a new Rolls-Royce: You can live through the ride, but it doesn't do much for your peace of mind, which is what is at stake here. More than anything else, solitude is about achieving peace of mind, tranquility of spirit and clarity of thought. Loneliness is random; solitude is ritual. Loneliness is black coffee and late-night television; solitude is herb tea and soft music. Solitude, quality solitude, is an assertion of self-worth, because only in the stillness can we hear the truth of our own unique voices. Yet my associations with solitude have not always been so sweet. Solitude was something I backed into in self-defense when my other options seemed to run toward babbling at strangers on the telephone and weeping unexpectedly in the grocery store.

The end of my ten-year marriage found me in my own apartment. I was spending a lot of time alone, but my thoughts and spirit were more scattered than ever, and spending time by myself terrified me. Alone with my thoughts? Forget it! I became short-tempered and confused. My energy level fluctuated between manic and nonexistent. I was making decisions on my own for the first time, and I was uncertain about them. I was floundering and I knew it, but I couldn't find an organized way out of the chaos. Then one day I turned on the radio, and there was Billie Holiday, singing like a dream, and my mother's voice came back to me: *"...someplace quiet to collect my thoughts. That's the solitude I was talking about..."*

Suddenly it made sense to me. I recognized in me the same yearning for solitude that I had heard in my mother's singing all those years ago. I wanted to know my own thoughts -- away from all those absolutely-certain-about-everything male voices I knew. I wanted to hear myself singing. I began thinking about trying to structure some time alone with myself.

But how to begin? I knew structure was critical to the success of my quest; otherwise I'd use the time to sort the laundry or balance my checkbook. I decided to focus on creating a conducive environment.

Since the moon has always been connected with myths of female magic and power, the first day of the next full moon seemed like a good time to start. The time of day wasn't critical, but I knew I needed at least one uninterrupted hour. I made sure I had on hand things that were soothing and pleasurable -- fragrant bath oils, fresh sheets on the bed, sweet incense and raspberry tea. When the appointed day and hour arrived, I dropped my daughter off with her father, unplugged my telephone, ran a hot bath, slid in up to my chin and waited.

I have to admit I felt kind of silly, hunched down in the water with the moon shining in my window, waiting for immediate and magical revelations to occur. But I made myself be still. I closed my eyes and let my thoughts roam freely.

And roam they did -- to everything from my work, to my daughter, to my gentlemen friends, to my health, to my friends and back again. I didn't try to determine the right or wrong of anything that popped into my mind. I simply tried to be the same open, non-judgmental ear for myself I try to be for those who are closest to me. And at the end of an hour, I was refreshed and energized in a way I hadn't been before. I was amazed, but still skeptical.

So the next day I tried it again, this time sitting in my rocking chair just before the sun came up and my house came alive. I sat still for half an hour, and by the time I went to wake my daughter, I felt centered and ready for the day. I began to look forward to these times of solitude. I felt myself getting stronger and more peaceful as the weeks went by. Solitude became a regular part of my life. But what did I do with all this newfound, peaceful energy? I fell in love.

Suddenly the thought of spending quality time alone was replaced with a desire to be with the man I love. The benefits of solitude paled when stacked beside the excitement of an evening with him. Besides, I'd decided that all that contemplation, thought and listening to myself were only preparations for true companionship with A Significant Other. The healing effects of the last few months had lulled me into a false sense of security.

So I took my friend into my solitude hours and let him share the bath and smell the incense and replace my tea with a glass of chilled champagne, and it was wonderful. For a while. But then something started happening. His voice began to fuel my dreams. The beating of his heart became the rhythm I was seeking. And the *she*, who speaks so softly even loving male voices overpower her, began to slip away.

But I was not prepared to let her go. I had finally learned to depend on her, to listen to her, to trust her wisdom and her courage. I realized that the ear I wanted to bend with the particulars of my life was *my own*. The advice and counsel I needed most regularly were *my own*. I needed my own company, my own guidance and "someplace quiet to collect my thoughts" as much when I was happy as when I was sad, maybe even more.

So I assured my friend that this "solitude thing" was not a rejection of him, but a reclaiming and nurturing of a part of myself that was critical to everything I was or hoped to be. I closed the door upon myself, brewed another cup of tea, took a deep breath and sat down in my same old place to watch the moon rise. And the quiet became the stillness and the stillness became the peace and the peace became a path to a new way of life. I know my mother would understand.

GOOD BROTHER BLUES

[Author's Note: This piece was written for performance and premiered at the second National Black Arts Festival in August of 1990 as part of the series "Just Us Theater Presents Live at Club Zebra!" The piece was staged with video by Zaron W. Burnett, Jr.]

I spend a lot of time talking to my sisters, and in between raising our children and earning our livings and struggling for our freedom and loving our womenfriends and building a new world, we sometimes -- every now and then -- talk about the brothers.

Invariably the discussion moves from vivid descriptions of the various ways in which the brothers stray far and wide from our definition of what constitutes "a good brother", to wistful expressions of disbelief at the unrelenting shortage in this area, to a resigned sigh and the unspoken question of why there seem to be so many more good *sisters* than there are good *brothers.*

Now I will admit that these are complex questions to consider, but how can we arrive at the correct position on the issues of the day without confronting them? Is Marian Barry, for example, a "good brother" with a few personal problems, under siege from the forces of racism and evil, *or* a physically abusive, womanhater who regularly lied to his wife, manipulated his female employees and acquaintances, and backhanded his lover so hard he knocked her down before she had ever even *met* any FBI agents?

See what I mean about the complexity of the questions? But I am optimistic. I believe we can work it out. I believe we have to and that time is getting very short...

So, as part of that move toward clarity, I offer the following Report from the Front Lines as part of my continuing, long term examination of *whatever* it is that is going on between black men and black women.

My latest research indicates that part of the problem is that most brothers don't have any clear idea of what *we* think a good brother is. This means that there is a strong possibility that it is their confusion, not their ill will, that makes the gulf so wide between us and them.

Perhaps the problem is that we haven't given them a current, updated, cross-referenced definition to work with.maybe they are just sort of marking time, following their own black, male instincts, until we reach consensus and begin to spread the good word.

And maybe, in this terrible vacuum of values and standards they are simply following the lead of their white male counterparts, a thuggish group of violent, homophobic, womanhating, n'er do wells, whose commitment to sexism is matched only by their absolute dedication to racism and their continuing quest to control as much of the world as they can get their greedy, warmongering hands on.

Assuming this is the case -- and I know this comes under the category of *giving the brothers the benefit of the doubt,* but we have almost *nothing* left to lose and *everything* to gain -- so assuming this is the case,I think it is time we put forward a working definition of *who* and *what* we are looking for.

We are looking for a good brother.

We are looking for a righteous brother. A *real righteous brother.* Not one of those singing white guys who made the loss of love sound so intensely intense that you had to fall in love every time the record came on.

We are looking for a real righteous brother.An all grown up, ain't scared of nuthin', and knows it's time to save the race righteous brother.

A good father / good husband / good lover / good worker / good warrior / serious revolutionary righteous brother.

A tuck the baby in at night and accept equal responsibility for child raising *and* household maintenance chores righteous brother.

A generate a regular paycheck *or* provide evidence of mutually agreed upon, full-time alternative service to the race or to the family, such as playing a saxophone or writing novels, or providing community defense, or taking primary responsibility for children's nurturing and education righteous brother.

A read a book and play a tune and dance your slow dance sweet and low down righteous brother.

A love black women, protect black children and never hit a woman righteous brother.

A turn the t.v. off and let's talk instead righteous brother.

A turn the t.v. off and let's make love instead righteous brother.

A stay at home cause that's where you wanna be righteous brother.

A brother who can *listen.*

A brother who can *teach.*

A brother who can *change.* For the better.

A brother who can *move.* Toward the center of the earth.

A brother who is not intimidated or confused by the *power* and the *magic* of women.

We are looking for a righteous brother. What we used to call *a good brother.*

A brother who loves his people.

A brother who doesn't hit or holler or shoot or stab or grab or shove or kick or shake or slap or punch women or children.

A brother who doesn't call women *hoes, bitches, skanks, pussies, dykes, sluts, cunts, etc.etc.etc.*

A brother who knows there is no such thing as a rape joke.

A brother who uses condoms without being asked.

A brother who doesn't call sex *screwing.*

A brother who knows that time and tenderness are more important than size and speed and that reciprocity is everything.

A brother who knows that permission must be gained at every step before proceeding.

A brother who doesn't describe the details of an intimate heterosexual encounter by saying, *"Man, I knocked the bottom out of it."* Or: *"I fucked her brains out."* Or: *"I drew blood from that bitch."*

A brother who says: *"I made her feel good. I showed her how much I love and cherish her."*

A brother who says: *"I rubbed warm oil on her."*

A brother who says: *" I kissed every part of her I could kiss."*

A brother who says: *" I made her feel so safe and happy and free that she fell asleep in my arms and her heart beat sounded like the ocean after a storm..."*

We are looking for a *real* good brother.

We are looking for a brother who will turn the ships around.

Now I know the whole boat question is a Serious Manhood Thing, and I know how dangerous it can be to offer an opinion about any topic that falls within their sacred circle, but I'll risk it for the sake of clarification. We can't afford to have any further confusion on these questions of what does and does not constitute manhood. Not from our side anyway.

In doing the necessary research to put forward our working definition of a good brother, it came to my attention that some brothers feel that we, their sisters, are giving mixed signals when it comes to the manhood thing. We want, they say, all the protection and safety offered by a strong man, but we are unwilling to accept the presence of the warrior's heart.

We, they say, are responsible for any confusion that exists on the manhood question; *we* are the ones, they say, that counsel caution instead of courage; diplomacy instead of defense.

They say that when the ships pulled up on the shores of Africa and the slavers came ashore to look for us, that *we* were the ones who held them back; the ones who told them that it might be dangerous to go down to the water's edge.

We were the ones, they say, who encouraged them to stay at home, telling them how worried we would be if they went down there with the other warriors to turn the ships around. Assuring them that if they just sat here by the fire with us, the white folks would probably change their minds and go away all by themselves. They say that's the reason why they didn't turn the ships around. Because they thought *we* didn't want them to.

Assuming this is a correct presentation of herstorical fact *(and I am unconvinced)* it is clearly one of the greatest examples of miscommunication in all of human herstory and one we should avoid repeating at all costs.

So let it be known that we are looking for a brother who will turn the ships around.

A brother who will go into the crack house and turn the ships around.

A brother who will go to the places where it is open season on our children and turn the ships around.

A brother who will hear the screams of sisters beaten to death by the men who say they love them and turn the ships around.

A brother who will hear the whimper of our babies born with AIDS and turn the ships around.

A brother who will see the people sleeping on the street and turn the ships around.

A brother who will remember how freedom feels and turn the ships around.

A brother who will gather with the warriors and march down to the edge of the sea and turn the ships around / turn the ships around / turn the ships around / *and this time,* turn the ships around...

MEAN TO BE FREE

don't wanna be half/thing.
don't wanna be less/than/thing.
don't wanna be confined/defined/refined.
don't wanna be inna box.
don't wanna be yawn/okay/but/no/time/for/that/now/thing.
don't wanna be guilt/thing.
don't wanna be screech/thing.
don't wanna be finger/point/thing.
don't wanna be weeping/thing/fussing/thing/cussing/thing.
wanna be free / wanna be free / wanna be free.
twenty-four hours a day/
seven days a week/
fifty-two weeks a year/
straight up, dead ahead,
no breaks, no tears, no fears free!
mean to be free /
mean to be free /
mean to be free...

About the Author

PEARL CLEAGE is an Atlanta-based writer and performance artist. She is the Artistic Director of Just Us Theater Company, Editor of CATALYST Magazine and a regular columnist in *The Atlanta Tribune.* Her work appears regularly in ESSENCE Magazine and other periodicals. A graduate of Spelman College and currently a member of the faculty there, her work has been supported by The National Endowment for the Arts, The Coca-Cola Foundation, The Georgia Council on the Arts, The Atlanta Bureau of Cultural Affairs and AT&T. She collaborates regularly with writer/performer Zaron W. Burnett, Jr. in their ongoing series "Live at Club Zebra!" Pearl is the author of The Brass Bed and Other Stories, (Third World Press, 1990), and the mother of one daughter, Deignan Njeri. MAD AT MILES: A BLACKWOMAN'S GUIDE TO TRUTH is the first of a series of Pearl's works to be published by The Cleage Group, Inc.